I0411523

HEART AND MINDS (Vol.3)
50 DIVERSITY AND EQUALITY CASE STUDIES

COPYRIGHT NOTICE

Copyright © 2015 D. Constantine-Simms (The Author)

Copyright © 2015 Think Doctor Publication (Publisher)

All rights reserved. No part of this publication may be reproduced, distributed, or transmitted in any form or by any means, including photocopying, recording, or other electronic or mechanical methods, without the prior written permission of the publisher.

ISBN-13: 978-1507850350

ISBN-10: 1507850352

ABOUT THE EDITOR

D. Constantine-Simms is an Occupational Psychologist, Counselling Psychologist and a qualified Therapeutic Career Coach. He is also as freelance print and photojournalist, whose work is regularly submitted and distributed by photo agencies such as Corbis Images and Demotix. His articles and images have appeared in British and international publications such as the Word (Canada) The Big Issue, The Guardian, The Voice Newspaper, Miami Times, and many other publications. Constantine-Simms has previously edited the following books and Co-edited Teachers for the Future (1995) The Greatest Taboo: Homosexuality in Black Communities (2001) Hip Hop Had a Dream: Vol. 1 the Artful Movement (2008)Constantine-Simms is the recipient of the 2001 Lambda Award for Best Anthology for his book: The Greatest Taboo: Homosexuality in Black Communities (2001).

DIVERSITY & EQUALITY

HEART AND MINDS (Vol.3)
50 DIVERSITY AND EQUALITY CASE STUDIES

Hearts and Minds (Vol.1)
A Resource Book of More Than 60 Learning Activities to Affirm Diversity and Promote Equality

OVERVIEW

Hearts and Minds is an excellent resource manual that's been designed to encourage participants by way of interactive exercises, mini-case studies and role play to achieve the following learning objectives.

1)   Identify different types of discrimination
2)   Examine their own cultural backgrounds
3)   Raise awareness about prejudices and preconceptions
4)   Empower a sense of human dignity and social responsibility
5)   Recognize how cultural differences may impact behaviour.
6)   Reduce conflict.
7)   Acknowledge Stereotypes
8)   Identify individual and organizational attitudes towards diversity and equality.

In order to achieve these objectives this resource book has been divided into the following eight sections.

1)   Prejudice and Discrimination
2)   The Role of Media Section
3)   Lookism
4)   Language and Diversity
5)   Diversity and Equality
6)   Power Privilege and Status
7)   Stereotype Thinking
8)   Cultural Diversity

Each activity is generally presented in the following format with variations:

1)   Name, to identify the exercise
2)   Brief description of the purpose of the exercise
3)   Normal time allotment
4)   Equipment required
5)   Consumable materials needed
6)   Procedures suggesting how the exercise should be conducted
7)   Short conclusion section
8)   Helpful trainers notes

This resource book does not assume that diversity and equality consultants are familiar with organizational theory. However, it is incumbent on users of this resource book to adopt the exercise accordingly with a view to ensuring they are have a good understanding of the relevant theories behind each exercise, in that their clients can benefit by ensuring that learning aims and objectives are achieved.

ISBN-13: 978-1499131758

HEART AND MINDS (Vol.3)
50 DIVERSITY AND EQUALITY CASE STUDIES

Hearts and Minds (Vol. 2)
A Resource Book of More Than 30 Learning Activities to Affirm Diversity and Promote Equality

OVERVIEW

Hearts and Minds (2) is an excellent resource manual that's been designed to encourage participants by way of interactive exercises, mini-case studies and role play to achieve the following outcomes:
1) Identify different types of discrimination
2) Examine their own cultural backgrounds
3) Raise awareness about prejudices and preconceptions
4) Empower a sense of human dignity and social responsibility
5) Recognize how cultural differences may impact behaviour.
6) Reduce conflict.
7) Acknowledge Stereotypes
8) Identify individual and organizational attitudes towards diversity and equality.

The activities have been divided into the following eight sections
1) Gender Discrimination
2) Disability Discrimination
3) Sexuality
4) Transexual/Transgender
5) Racial Discrimination
6) Ageism
7) Religious Beliefs

Each activity is generally presented in the following format with variations:
1) Name, to identify the exercise
2) Brief description of the purpose of the exercise
3) Normal time allotment
4) Equipment required
5) Consumable materials needed
6) Procedures suggesting how the exercise should be conducted
7) Short conclusion section
8) Helpful trainers notes

Furthermore, this activity book encourages the use of interactive exercises, mini-case studies and role plays in which participants can actively engage in situations that help participants deal with diversity and equality issues privately, in the workplace, as well as the wider community.

ISBN-13: 9781499351149

PAPERBACK BOOKS EDITED BY AUTHOR

Constantine-Simms has previously edited the following books:

- Rice & Peas For The Soul 2 (2015)
- Rice & Peas For The Soul 1 (2014)
- The Greatest Taboo: Homosexuality in Black Communities (2001)
- Hip Hop Had a Dream: Vol. 1 The Artful Movement (2008)
- 12 Years A Slave
- Behind The Scenes
- Thirty Years A Slave,...
- Incidents in the Life of a Slave...
- Fifty Years In Chains
- From Bondage To Freedom
- Hearts and Minds (Vol. 1)
- Hearts and Minds (Vol. 2)

E-BOOKS BY AUTHOR

- How to Get Motivated
- How to Plan For A New Career
- How to Develop Unstoppable Confidence
- Successful Interviews: Making The Most Of The Interview
- The Interview Guide: A Job Interview Is No Different Than Finding The Right Partner
- The Structure and Application of Cognitive Behavioural Therapy
- How to Think Critically
- Mentoring As A Workforce Development Strategy
- The Counselling Process In Six Stages: A Basic Guide For Psychologists Counsellors and Psychotherapists
- Linking Emotional Intelligence To Effective Leadership
- Stress Management
- A Critique Of Executive Coaching Through The Psychodynamic Window
- Otto Kernberg's Theory of Personality: Pathological Narcissism and Borderline Personality Disorders
- Personality Development and Confidence Building
- The Psychology of the Courtroom
- How To Improve Your Communication Skills
- How Employment Assessment Centres Work
- Linking Emotional Intelligence To Effective Leadership
- Stress Management Leading Career Development and Employability
- The History of Psychological Testing
- Have You Ever Thought of Becoming A Life Coach
- Successful Interviews
- The 360 Degree Feedback System Is By Far The Best Performance Assessment Tool By Far.

CONTENTS

COPYRIGHT NOTICE 2

ABOUT THE EDITOR 3

PAPERBACK BOOKS EDITED BY AUTHOR 7

E-BOOKS BY AUTHOR 8

INTRODUCTION 14

SEXISM 15

SEXISM IN THE CITY 16

SEXIST INTERVIEW QUESTIONS 19

IN TASKS AT WORK 20

SEXUALLY HARASSED AT SCHOOL 22

NAKED VIEW 24

YOU CAN'T TOUCH THIS! 25

PROVISION OF GOODS AND SERVICES 26

DIFFERENT BENEFITS 28

REDUNDANCY 29

LACK OF EXPERIENCE 30

EQUAL PAY 31

MALES SEXISM APPLICANT PREFERRED 32

HARASSED WHILE PREGNANT 33

UNDISCLOSED PREGNANCY 35

NO WOMEN ON OUR SHIP! 37

MATERNITY LEAVE 39

DISABILITY 41

COPING WITH MY CAREER 42

ASSUMED IMPAIRMENT (HIV) 44

IMPAIRMENT DISCRIMINATION IN WORK 46

RELIGION 47

FIVE TIMES A DAY 48

RAMADAM 49

ATHEIST 50

TURBAN ISSUE 51

BANGLE ISSUES 52

AGEISM 53

AGE DISCRIMINATION IN A SHOP 54

A GENERATION APART 55

AGE IN WORK 56

COLD SHOULDERED 58

WORKING PAST RETIREMENT 59

YOUNG AT HEART 60

TOO YOUNG 61

TRANSGENDER: HIDDEN TRANNY 62

TRANSGENDER..63

NO STOP AND SEARCH 64

NO FLY TIME 66

NO SEARCHING ALLOWED..67

GENDER REASSIGNMENT 69

Fortnum v Suffolk County Council 69

RACISM..71

FACE DIDN'T FIT 72

PSYCHOMETRIC TESTING AND RACISM..........................74

LAZY ASIAN 76

ALL LEBANESE MEN ARE TROUBLE 78

EFFECT OF RACIAL BIAS..79

MISINFORMATION 81

STEREOTYPICAL ASSUMPTION 83

WHO ARE YOU CALLING "BOY"?......................................85

MY FIRST NAME..86

HE AINT NO DOG 87

SEXUALITY..88

PARENTAL STATUS...89

HOMOPHOBIA 91

DISCLOSURE..92

HOMOPHOBIC ABUSE...94

DON'T TELL! 95

IT'S JUST FUN! 96

CROSS DRESSER 97

BE IT BUT DON'T FLAUNT IT! 98

ADVERTISEMENTS 99

DISMISSAL 102

HEART AND MINDS (Vol.3)
50 DIVERSITY AND EQUALITY CASE STUDIES

HEART AND MINDS (Vol. 3)
50 DIVERSITY AND EQUALITY CASE STUDIES

INTRODUCTION

How many times have you as a trainer and consultant, struggled to find suitable case studies? How often have you conducted a training session, in which delegates are reluctant to disclose their experiences of injustice and inequality? Well look no further, **Hearts and Minds 3** is a selection of 50 diversity and equality case studies, which covers a range of issues linked to Sexism, Disability, Racism, Sexuality Ageism and more.

Hearts and Minds (3) 50 Diversity and Equality Case Studies offers learners, and consultants the opportunity to analyze and reflect upon a variety of realistic case studies relating to personal, professional and social justice. The case studies may vary in length, however, each case presents a complex but common scenario in which an inequality and an injustice has taken place. These cases studies enable learners, to practice the process of considering a range of contextual factors, including assessing their own prejudices, and how such biases determine how they interact in the wider community. Furthermore, this resource tool provides consultants and trainers with an excellent opportunity to facilitate a learning environment, which enables learners to offer their opinions while being empowered to develop real strategies which can address issues of prejudice and discrimination without the use of legal action where possible.

SEXISM

SEXISM IN THE CITY

Susan, 22, was becoming depressed following a stream of sexist harassment from her male colleagues. Finally she took control of the situation though, and proved that their behaviour was unacceptable.

"I had always dreamed of a high flying city career so when I graduated I worked hard to get a job in a well-respected financial institution. I knew I had the skills to do well and was really excited to get started.

"Obviously I was aware that it is a very male dominated industry but I had 2 brothers so was used to being one of the guys and it didn't phase me in the slightest. I made sure that I dressed professionally and was ready to give them a run for their money.

Bad start

"The other men in my group were hostile to me from the moment that I started. I found out later that I had taken a role that they thought was going to one of their friends so I think they resented me.

"To begin with they did not make any sexist comments but were just generally cold and unhelpful. I naively thought that I just had to prove myself and their attitudes towards me would turn around."

Unfortunately, things soon went from bad to worse for Kirsty, and however hard she worked, she couldn't break through.

"It started in a subtle way to begin with, with the odd comment here and there. I thought I was just being sensitive and put up with it. However, soon my male colleagues were making overtly sexual jokes around me and insinuating things that made me feel very uncomfortable.

"It was past the point of making a joke of it so I tried to talk to the ringleader and ask why he was being like that. He played innocent and apologised for any 'misinterpretation' but nothing changed. In fact, I think he just wound up his friends more and the harassment became more frequent."

Taking action

"Their behaviour was getting to me so much that I dreaded going into work and slipped into a spate of depression. I knew I couldn't let them win so I finally plucked up the courage to do something about it. I started keeping notes of everything they said and did so that I had a good record.

"Then I made an appointment and approached my boss about it. I expected him to be unsympathetic but actually he took my complaint very seriously. The grievance was dealt with in-house and the men received disciplinary action and were moved to different departments.

"It felt great that somebody was on my side and that I had stood up for myself. Since then I have been treated as an equal by my new colleagues and am happy and thriving in my role.

I would advise anyone who is being discriminated against to find the courage to speak up. It's not your fault, it shouldn't be tolerated and you can get back your life and your confidence back.

Suggested Questions

1. What was wrong with is suggestion that men work at the back?
2. Did the manager make an unreasonable request?
3. Realistically, what could the manger have done to ensure that all his employees were being treated fairly?

Debriefing: (10 minutes)

Sum up the debriefing with a presentation of stereotypes, prejudices, discrimination and exclusion especially sexism.

SEXIST INTERVIEW QUESTIONS

Rachel, a single mother, attends a job interview for a position as an office junior. After answering all the questions without any problems, Wendy, the interviewer and office manager, asked Rachel whether she was single or in a relationship, or had any children.

Suggested Questions

1. Should she lie and say that she does not have children?
2. Should Wendy make a complaint?
3. What if Wendy was Wayne a single Father, would the employer be justified in asking these questions.
4. Should Wendy ask what the question about her marital or maternal status has to do with the job?
5. In plenary each group is asked to present their arguments

SEXISM IN TASKS AT WORK

Christie and Ben, both 16 years old, apply for casual jobs at a fast food store. The store manager gets Christie working on the register, and Ben working in the kitchen.

Christie and Ben ask if they can swap jobs. The manager tells them that he prefers girls to work on the register because it 'looks better', and the boys should work in the kitchen because 'they're faster and don't complain about the hot conditions'.

Christie and Ben both think this is unfair, but the manager tells them if they don't like the work he has offered them they can find themselves another job.

What would you do if you were Christie or Ben?
Options
   a. Quit your job and find another one.
   b. Put up with it. It's no big deal.
   c. Get advice on what you can do.

Split the participants into 4 groups. Each group will be given this case to discuss and then present to the class.

Suggested Questions

1. What was wrong with is suggestion that men work at the back?
2. Did the manager make an unreasonable request?
3. Realistically, what could the manger have done to ensure that all his employees were being treated fairly?

Debriefing: (10 minutes)

Sum up the debriefing with a presentation of stereotypes, prejudices, discrimination and exclusion especially sexism.

SEXUALLY HARASSED AT SCHOOL

Caitlin is 17 years old and works part time in her local bakery. One day she and the other girls working there were told that all female employees now have to wear skirts instead of trousers. Some of Caitlin's duties include climbing up and down a ladder to get into the attic storage area, so she asks her manager if she can continue wearing trousers. Her manager says no, head office has decided that all females must now wear skirts. Caitlin replies if that's the case, she won't be climbing up and down the ladder to get supplies. Caitlin's manager threatens her with the sack if she won't do her job whilst wearing a skirt.

Instructions

What would you do if you were Caitlin?

Options

A. Quit your job and find another one

B. Get all the girls to keep wearing trousers

C. Get advice on what you can do

D. Wear a skirt and do your duties

Suggested Questions

1. Split the participants into 4 groups. Each group will be given this case to discuss and

2. Then present to the class.

3. Debriefing: (10 minutes)

4. Sum up the debriefing with a presentation of stereotypes, prejudices, discrimination and exclusion especially sexism.

NAKED VIEW

Brendan and Chloe are in the same year at school. Brendan asked Chloe out a couple of times, and each time she said no. She was flattered by the attention, but just didn't like him in that way. Brendan started some nasty rumours about things he and Chloe did together on a date, even though Chloe never went out with him. Chloe arrived at her locker one morning and there was a picture of a naked woman stuck to it, with Chloe's face photo-shopped onto the picture. Brendan and his friends were there laughing and making obscene gestures at her. One of the teachers walking past rolled her eyes and told them to 'grow up'.

What would you do if you were Chloe?

Options

A. Ignore the idiot. Brendan and his friends will get tired of it sooner or later.

B. Talk to a teacher or school counsellor about the problem.

C. Change schools.

D. Make a complaint of sexual harassment

YOU CAN'T TOUCH THIS!

Shaniqua is a media at an Ivy League university, does her work placement at a local urban radio station. Her supervisor there, Lee, asks her questions like 'Do you have a boyfriend?' and 'Have you ever been out with an older guy?' He insists that Alexis gives him her mobile number 'for OHS reasons' and sends her messages while she's at work as well as after work. The messages includes personal comments like 'You are looking gorgeous today' and 'what are you doing after work tonight?' Late one afternoon Mark brushes up against Alexis in the kitchen.

What would you do if you were Alexis?

Options:

A. Leave right then and there and refuse to go back to the radio station

B. Speak to the school's Work Placement Coordinator

C. Speak to Mark's supervisor

D. Tell Mark to leave you alone

E. Nothing - there's only two days left of work experience anyway

PROVISION OF GOODS AND SERVICES

Facts

A woman approached a company to purchase some goods. She asked to make an appointment for a company representative to visit, to do an in home quote. The woman alleges that she was told it would be necessary for her husband to be present at the quote. She asked the company if the same question would be asked of a man in the same situation and alleged that she was not given an answer.

In response the company said that its aim is to have all decision makers present when quotes are given so as to ensure that the correct information is relayed to all involved in the decision to purchase.

The company stated that single or widowed customers are given the option of having a friend with them when a quote is being provided.

In conciliation the company stated that they had not intended to act in a way that would be considered discriminatory.

The company acknowledged the problems associated with advising married customers to have all decision makers present and giving an option to other customers such as those who are single or widowed to have.

What would you do if you were Alexis?

Options:

A. Leave right then and there and refuse to go back to the radio station

B. Speak to the school's Work Placement Coordinator

C. Speak to Mark's supervisor

D. Tell Mark to leave you alone

E. Nothing - there's only two days left of work experience anyway

Decision

The company provided a written apology to the woman and agreed to develop and implement an anti-discrimination policy. This was done with the assistance of the Commission. After the conference the general manager of the company thanked the Commission for its assistance in bringing to their attention the potential problems with their previous practices. The company stated that they learned a great deal from being party to the complaint and that they will aim to avoid any further complaints being lodged in future.

DIFFERENT BENEFITS

Facts

Brenda' was a manager in a trucking company but received less pay and fewer benefits than her male colleagues performing the same duties. Unlike her male colleagues, Brenda did not receive a mobile phone, fuel cards or a car. The company demoted her from management, claiming male employees found it difficult to listen to females.

Instructions

Brenda lodged a complaint of sex discrimination. At conciliation, Brenda's employer agreed she had been treated unfairly and they negotiated a settlement of £15,000 and a letter of regret.

REDUNDANCY

'Denise' worked in a textile factory. The company was bought out by another company and employees were told there would be some "downsizing" as a result. Denise was given a smaller redundancy payment than her male co-workers even though she had worked at the factory for the same length of time and on the same pay.

Suggested Questions

1. What are the issues in this case?
2. What are the potential outcomes of this situation?
3. What strategies can be implemented to address this situation?

Decision

Denise lodged a complaint of sex discrimination. After an investigation by the Commission, her employee agreed to adjust her redundancy package so that it equalled her male colleagues.

LACK OF EXPERIENCE

Fact

'Jenny' was the only woman employed in a male dominated industry. When senior positions became available she was not considered for promotion despite many years in the industry. Males were given precedence over her even though they did not have the same level of experience. She raised her concerns with her employer and shortly after her work performance was criticised and she was sacked.

Suggested Questions

1. What are the issues in this case?
2. What are the potential outcomes of this situation?
3. What strategies can be implemented to address this situation?

Decision

Jenny lodged a complaint of sex discrimination. At conciliation, Jenny and her employer negotiated a settlement of $14,000.

EQUAL PAY

Fact

'Martha', a despatch supervisor, discovered that male Despatch Supervisors were on a higher wage package and received greater benefits than she did. She also claimed that she was moved out of the Despatch Supervisor role in an attempt to force her resignation. She was told that drivers found it difficult to listen to females. She resigned from the position after a year.

Suggested Questions

1. What are the issues in this case?
2. What are the potential outcomes of this situation?
3. What strategies can be implemented to address this situation?

Answer

Martha lodged a complaint of sex discrimination. At conciliation, her employer acknowledged that Martha had been treated unfairly and agreed to pay her $15,000 as an ex-gratia payment and issued a statement of regret.

MALES APPLICANT PREFERRED

Fact

'Debbie' got a job in a factory. After three days on the job, her new boss called her into his office and said he had decided that her job would be better filled by a man. He then dismissed her on the spot.

Suggested Questions

1. What are the issues in this case?
2. What are the potential outcomes of this situation?
3. What strategies can be implemented to address this situation?

Decision

Debbie lodged a complaint of sex discrimination. After an investigation by the Commission, her employer agreed that she had been treated unfairly. Debbie did not feel that she wanted to continue working for this employer, and settled for a written apology and a job reference.

HARASSED WHILE PREGNANT

Fact

A woman complained to the Commission that after informing her employer she was pregnant, her supervisor made numerous comments suggesting she would need to finish work. Suggestions were also made that her position would not be available after her baby's birth due to restructuring. The supervisor had placed documents in the woman's "In tray", amongst other paper work, which related to maternity leave and how to terminate an employee.

On finding these documents she took them to her solicitor who in turn wrote to the employer advising that a complaint would be lodged with the Commission. The employer, on receiving the solicitor's letter stood her down on full pay, pending an investigation, alleging the woman removed confidential documents from his office.

Her solicitor then lodged a complaint of victimization and discrimination on the ground of pregnancy with the Commission. All parties agreed to informal conciliation by the Commission with a view to avoiding the formal complaint process. At conciliation she was offered reinstatement, but because of the dispute the woman felt the future working environment would not be tolerable.

Suggested Questions

1. What are the issues in this case?

2. What are the potential outcomes of this situation?

3. What strategies can be implemented to address this situation?

Decision

The employer agreed to accept her resignation and pay all associated entitlements. The employer also agreed to pay her legal costs regarding the dispute, provide a reference and pay £3,500 for the distress, pain and suffering she experienced.

UNDISCLOSED PREGNANCY

Fact

A woman engaged to work on a temporary contract (six months) knew she was pregnant when she was employed and did not disclose the fact to the potential employer as the baby was not due until one month after the contract would be completed. She was of the view that she would be able to fulfill the job requirements during the contract term. The woman hoped that the employer would recognize her good work and would want to retain her as an employee after the contract ended as she only planned to have 12 weeks away from work when the baby was born.

At the conference the company advised that it had a practice of keeping employees after the expiration of a contract where it is possible and suitable to both sides. Approximately six weeks after commencing work the woman advised the employer that she was pregnant.

A manager advised the woman that he was disappointed that she had not 'come clean' at the job interview and that he wished she had told him up front. The woman claimed her supervisor then began treating her poorly.

She felt forced to resign (four weeks before the end of the contract period) by pressure put on her by the supervisor about when she was going to leave. The woman rejoined the workforce in a similar role with a different company when the baby was 12 weeks old.

Suggested Questions

1. What are the issues in this case?

2. What are the potential outcomes of this situation?

3. What strategies can be implemented to address this situation?

Decision

At the conference the supervisor said he had enquired about when the woman was going to finish working and had suggested she should discuss it with her husband as he had concerns for her and the baby's health.

NO WOMEN ON OUR SHIP!

Facts

A woman who had been employed in the office of a water transport business for a number of years, decided to seek employment with the same company as deck-hand. She expressed long-term plans to gain a Captain's licence. She alleged she was made to feel unwelcome by her male co-workers who commented to her that the work would be too heavy and dirty for her. The male co-workers conceded over time that she was able to perform the duties of the position as well as they could.

Because of a down-turn in business the company was forced to remove a service which resulted in a reduction in work hours for deck-hands. As a consequence her rostered water-time was shortened resulting in loss of hours and loss of training and career opportunities. She alleged her complaints to the company about unfair treatment by favouring male staff in the rostering times were ignored.

In her view, the apparent necessity to reduce hours was unfairly distributed between her and her male colleagues. Her chosen career to aspire to Captaincy, she intimated, was seriously jeopardised. In conciliation the respondents conceded that there were no female deck-hands, acknowledged that the comments about work being too heavy and dirty for her were made, and that this may have influenced the distribution of work.

Suggested Questions

1. What are the issues in this case?

2. What are the potential outcomes of this situation?

3. What strategies can be implemented to address this situation?

Decision

The complaint was settled by conciliation with payment of $12,000 compensation, a written apology and agreement that the company would undertake training on anti-discrimination.

MATERNITY LEAVE

Facts

A woman alleged discrimination by her team leader, on the basis of parental status, after taking maternity leave, and in the process of returning to work.

She alleged, among other things, that the team leader pressured her to familiarise herself with a manual while she was on maternity leave, (when other staff were given time at work to do this)

She alleged felt that she was pressured to stop breastfeeding her baby as it would interfere with the travel involved in her work; that the pressure to stop breastfeeding caused her to develop severe mastitis and other medical complications

She also alleged that she was denied a one off request to bring her baby to work for a few hours as she had no other child care options.

The continue to argue; that she was denied a request to take her husband and child on an overseas conference at their own expense (while other interstate colleagues attended the conference with spouses and children); that the above culminated in her having to take sick leave and then her being constructively dismissed.

Suggested Questions

1. What are the issues in this case?

2. What are the potential outcomes of this situation?

3. What strategies can be implemented to address this situation?

The complainant was highly qualified and received a wage package including a salary, sales incentives, company care, mobile phone and computer.

Decision

The matter was resolved with a financial settlement of $100, 000 comprising loss of income and medical expenses, and a personal reference.

DISABILITY

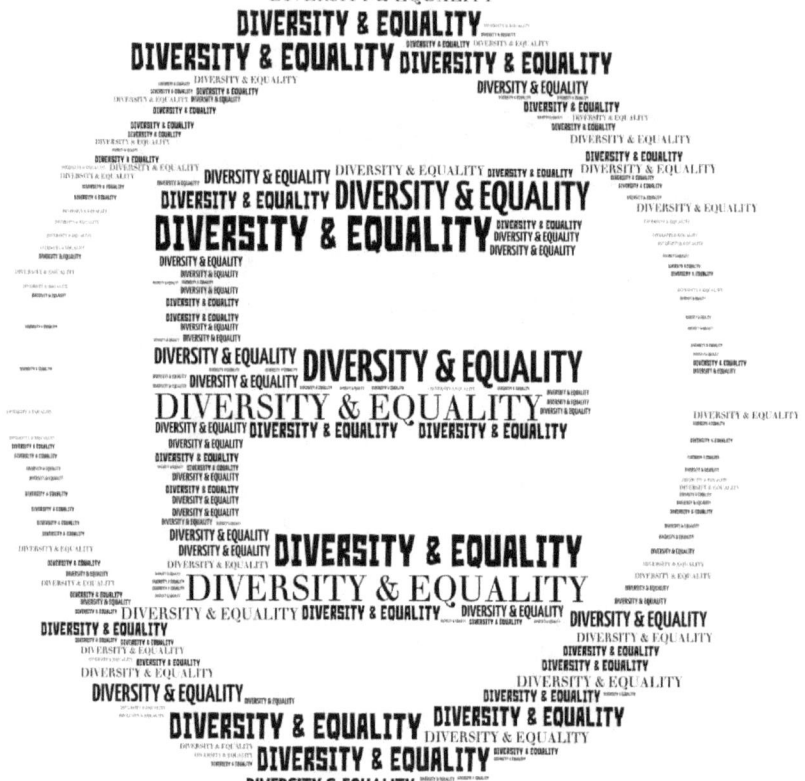

COPING WITH MY CAREER

Alex, 42, has been in a wheelchair since he was 7. He says that most of his experiences at work have been good, although some companies still have a long way to go. "I have been in wheelchair for most of my life and attended a mainstream school so I have never thought of myself as different or even disabled. Yes, some things are a little harder for me, but with a little bit of thought and some adaptations I can manage to do most things an able-bodied person could. "When I left school I started working in IT. My first employer was very forward thinking for the time and made a great effort to make sure that all my needs were met and that I wasn't treated any differently from any other employee. I am very glad that they were my first experience of the workplace as it allowed me to see what is possible."

Bad experiences

"When I was in my late 20s I was looking for a bit of a change and got a job as an IT training manager in a small company.

As soon as I started though, I realised that it was a mistake. I think they took me on because they needed to show they had filled their quota of disabled people rather than actually wanting me there.

Nothing was set up conveniently for me and it was a constant challenge to get things changed.

I also found myself excluded from certain meetings because access for the wheelchair was impossible and had decisions made over my head. Eventually I took them to an employment tribunal and won, which was a good boost to my confidence."

Questions:

1. What are the issues in this case?
2. What are the longevity issues?
3. Did the Carol handle the situation well?
4. What are the potential outcomes of this situation?
5. What strategies can be implemented to address this situation?

ASSUMED IMPAIRMENT (HIV)

A man had worked for some time at a local supermarket without disclosing to his co-workers that he was gay. His colleagues eventually suspected that he was gay, after he had been seen out at a gay nightclub, and in an attempt to put an end to rumour, the man told his colleagues that he was gay. After declaring this, he was subjected to frequent jokes about his sexuality, rude remarks about the likelihood that he would pass on AIDS to his co-workers (even though he was not even HIV positive),and even threatened that he would be "bashed up " in the car park.

The man lodged a complaint on the basis of lawful sexual activity* and imputed impairment, against all of the co-workers who he alleged had

discriminated against him, and the employer. None of the co-workers denied what was alleged against them, but the employer denied that it was vicariously liable, arguing that it had taken reasonable steps to prevent the discrimination.

Suggested Questions

1. What are the issues in this case?

2. What are the potential outcomes of this situation?

3. What strategies can be implemented to address this situation?

Following a conciliation conference, the respondent employer agreed to pay the complainant an undisclosed sum, and to provide specific monetary and other assistance to him to relocate interstate.

IMPAIRMENT DISCRIMINATION IN WORK

The complainant alleged he was not employed because of his workers' compensation claim - because he ticked "yes" to a question about any 'Work cover' claims. The respondent said their policy was that they could not employ people who were currently receiving workers compensation unless they receive a clearance from Work cover.

The respondent provided documentary proof that they do employ people with prior workers compensation histories. There had obviously been some mis-communication. The respondent thought the complainant was currently receiving worker's compensation. According to the relevant legislation, he was barred from working while a workers' compensation claim is active.

In fact the complainant ticked "yes" only because he had a contested workers' compensation claim for a period in the past. The respondent showed he had employed a number of people who had worker's compensation histories.

Suggested Questions

1. What are the issues in this case?
2. What are the potential outcomes of this situation?
3. What strategies can be implemented to address this situation?

RELIGION

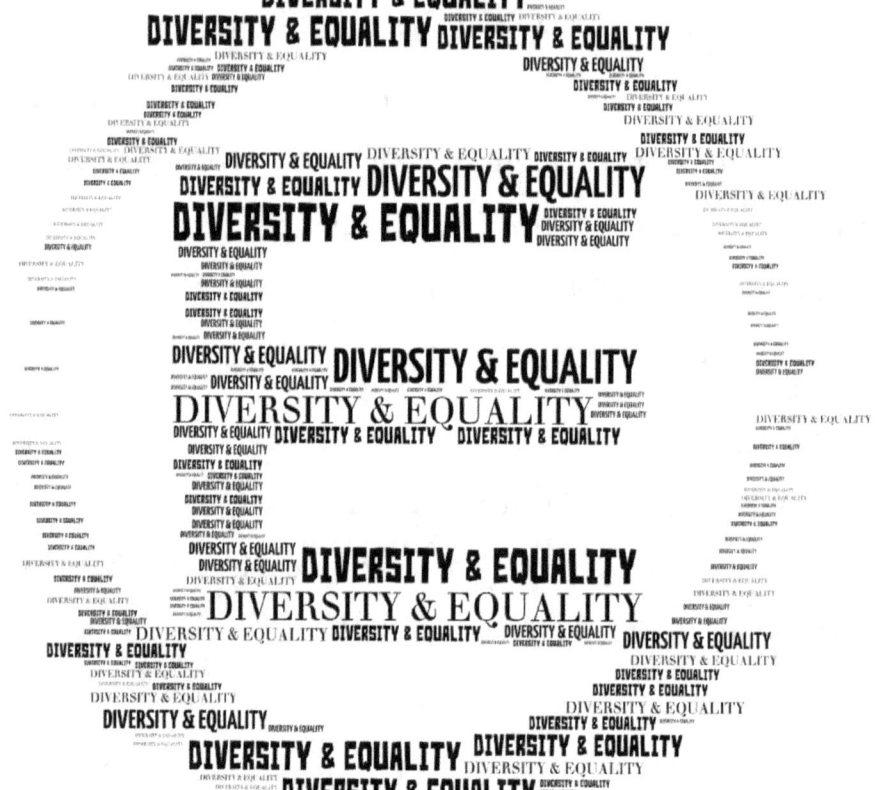

FIVE TIMES A DAY

Facts

Arif, who is Muslim, prays five times a day. At least two of these prayer sessions occur during work hours. Arif requests that his breaks be scheduled so he can pray at the appropriate times. His supervisor refuses, remarking "We pay you to work, not to pray. Leave the religious observances for your own time." Arif's supervisor carefully consider the request.

Suggested Question

1. What are the issues in this case?
2. What are the potential outcomes of this situation?
3. What strategies can be implemented to address this situation?
4. Identify the issues and list them in order of priority

Decision

Because Arif's request would not be costly, inefficient, unsafe, or negatively impact his co-workers' rights, the supervisor should have granted the request.

RAMADAM

A Muslim pupil asks for some flexibility in the school timetable to fit in with his religious commitments linked to the month of Ramadan. He asks not to have to participate in physical education classes held in the afternoon during the month of Ramadan when he will be fasting. This request is denied and he is required to attend PE classes in the afternoon. Another pupil requests some flexibility in the timetable to fit in with his confirmation classes at his church. He is permitted to leave class half an hour early on Fridays.

Suggested Questions

1. What are the issues in this case?
2. What are the potential outcomes of this situation?
3. What strategies can be implemented to address this situation?

Answer

This is likely to be unlawful direct discrimination against the first pupil because of religion or belief.

ATHEIST

A Catholic school excludes a pupil who has turned away from the Catholic faith and declared himself an atheist.

Suggested Questions

1. What are the issues in this case?
2. What are the potential outcomes of this situation?
3. What strategies can be implemented to address this situation?

Answer

This is likely to be unlawful direct discrimination because of religion or belief.

TURBAN ISSUE

A school requires male pupils to wear a cap as part of the school uniform. Although this requirement is applied equally to all pupils, it has the effect of excluding Sikh boys whose religion requires them to wear a turban.

1. What are the issues in this case?
2. What are the potential outcomes of this situation?
3. What strategies can be implemented to address this situation?

Answer

This is likely to be indirect discrimination because of religion and belief as it is unlikely that the school would be able to justify this action.

BANGLE ISSUES

A school instigates a policy that no jewellery should be worn. A young woman of the Sikh religion is asked to remove her Kara bangle in line with this policy, although the young woman explains that she is required by her religion to wear the bangle.

Suggested Questions

1. What are the issues in this case?
2. What are the potential outcomes of this situation?
3. What strategies can be implemented to address this situation?

Answer

This could be unlawful indirect discrimination on the grounds of religion and belief.

AGEISM

AGE DISCRIMINATION IN A SHOP

James and Liam, both 13 years old, go to a games shop after school. As they walk in they are told by the store manager to leave their school bags at the entrance of the shop, pointing to a sign next to the door displaying the shop's 'No school bags allowed inside' policy. Soon afterwards, they notice that a few older guys wearing business suits have been allowed to bring their bags into the store.

Instructions

What would you do if you were James or Liam?

Options

1. Walk out without buying anything
2. Ask the manager why others are allowed to bring their bags inside
3. Nothing

Suggested Questions

1. What are the issues in this case?
2. What are the potential outcomes of this situation?

A GENERATION APART

Carol has worked in the agency for thirteen years. A dedicated employee, she currently works in the human resources department. She was hired as an administrative assistant and has worked her way up in the agency over the years. Sally, a new employee in the department, is twenty-three years old. Carol supervises Sally's work and provides her with feedback. "When I was your age," Carol says, "I was working as a secretary. It took a long time for me to get where I am today. Your work is fine; Sally, but you don't put your heart into it. I think that's the problem with your generation — you're just not committed to your work."

Questions:

1. What are the issues in this case?
2. What are the longevity issues?
3. Did the Carol handle the situation well?
4. What are the potential outcomes of this situation?
5. What strategies can be implemented to address this situation?

AGE IN WORK

A woman alleged that she was dismissed from employment because of her age. When she was dismissed, the manager advised the woman that the business wanted to portray a certain image, and the woman didn't fit that image. The woman asked whether it was because of her age, and referred to the business recently employing young staff. After a lengthy discussion, the manager allegedly agreed that it was about the woman's age.

The manager offered to look for work for the woman in other locations of the business. The woman also alleged that in front of other employees, the manager had said he wanted "to make the place bop" and employ some young people he knew.

The employer said the woman was dismissed because of work performance issues. During a conciliation conference, the manager said he had discussed wanting to attract young people and clientele to the premises as they had high disposable income. The manager said he did not need young staff to attract young people to the premises, only staff with a "young attitude". The manager said that he did tell the woman he would try to arrange work for her in another location. He did not clarify why he would look for work for the woman when her work performance was allegedly not good.

Suggested Questions

1. What are the issues in this case?

2. What are the potential outcomes of this situation?

3. What strategies can be implemented to address this situation?

COLD SHOULDERED

A man in his 60s works with a team of colleagues in their 20s and 30s. The team, including the manager, often go out socialising but don't ask him along. He finds out that they discuss work issues during those trips and feels undervalued and left out.

Suggested Questions

1. What are the issues in this case?
2. What are the potential outcomes of this situation?
3. What strategies can be implemented to address this situation?

Result: This is harassment, even though it is unintended. The manager needs to consider office-based meetings to prevent his older worker being excluded. [source: Acas]

WORKING PAST RETIREMENT

A building contractor has set a retirement age of 60 because of the hard physical nature of the work, but one 60-year-old wants to challenge it.

Result: He can bring a claim for unfair dismissal and age discrimination if he can challenge the firm's "objective justification" for a retirement age of 60. The firm can't just say it's because of the nature of the work; they would have to explain in detail to the tribunal why this particular employee could not continue to do aspects of his work past 60.

Suggested Questions

1. What are the issues in this case?
2. What are the potential outcomes of this situation?
3. What strategies can be implemented to address this situation?

YOUNG AT HEART

I am interested in a job which requires someone who is "young, dynamic and energetic". I am over 50 years old, is this discrimination?

Suggested Questions

1. What are the issues in this case?
2. What are the potential outcomes of this situation?
3. What strategies can be implemented to address this situation?

Solution

If the employer is looking for a person younger than you this would be age discrimination unless the employer could show that it was necessary to appoint someone young. The company should not be making assumptions about older people's energy levels and their ability to do the job.

TOO YOUNG

I am in my early 20s. Unlike other employees I have not been promoted even though I have the required experience and qualifications. I think this is because my employer sees me as too young to handle the responsibility. Can they do this? This may be age discrimination. Your employer should not take your age into account when assessing you for promotion. They should make a decision based on the relevant skills and experience for the job. I am 55 and was rejected from a job as a sales assistant at a fashionable shop. They told me it was because they need to attract young customers and my face did not fit. Can they do this?

Suggested Questions

1. What are the issues in this case?
2. What are the potential outcomes of this situation?
3. What strategies can be implemented to address this situation?

Solution

Trying to attract young customers may be a legitimate business aim. But the shop should not reject you for this reason. The real job requirement should be that you have knowledge of the products and fashion awareness. You do not have to be young to have these, so this is likely to be age discrimination.

TRANSGENDER: HIDDEN TRANNY

Mills & Crown Prosecution Service v Marshall

In 1993, as a man, Ms Marshall successfully applied to join the Crown Prosecution Service. However, this job offer was withdrawn when she told them that she intended to take up the post as a woman. Ms Marshall did not make a claim to a tribunal about her treatment until 1996 following the ECJ judgement in the *P v S and Cornwall County Council* case (above) as until this time it had been thought that the SDA did not cover discrimination arising on the ground of being transsexual.

Suggested Questions

1. What are the issues in this case?
2. What are the potential outcomes of this situation?
3. What strategies can be implemented to address this situation?

Answer

The tribunal considered that it was just and equitable to hear the claim as Ms Marshall had acted quickly when she became aware that the SDA did cover discrimination as a transsexual person. The case settled on confidential terms after the time limit issue had been resolved.

TRANSGENDER

NO STOP AND SEARCH
M v West Midlands Police

M, who had undergone male to female gender reassignment, applied to join the West Midlands Police Force as a police constable. She passed the assessment procedures and was informed that she was suitable for appointment. As the school certificates she would have to supply would show that she had previously been a man, M decided to inform the West Midlands Police that she was transsexual. She subsequently received a rejection letter indicating that because of her gender reassignment, West Midlands Police considered that it would be inappropriate for her to carry out some of the duties of the post including searching suspects.

Suggested Questions

1. What are the issues in this case?

2. What are the potential outcomes of this situation?

3. What strategies can be implemented to address this situation?

Answer

The Industrial Tribunal found that discrimination on the grounds of gender reassignment did not come within the SDA/Equal Treatment Directive (ETD) but even if it did, West Midlands Police had a defence under s7 of the SDA which deals with genuine occupational qualifications and under Article 2.2 of the ETD. M's case was unsuccessful. Since this case was heard, the EAT has decided that the SDA and the ETD **does** cover discrimination on the grounds of being transsexual (see *P v S and Cornwall County Council* and *Chessington World of Adventure v Reed above*). However, since then, the SDA has been amended to make it lawful to discriminate against transsexual people in recruitment to a job if the work involves the holder conducting intimate searches pursuant to statutory powers as contained in, for example, The Police and Criminal Evidence Act.

NO FLY TIME
Malone v Ministry of Defence

Ms Malone was dismissed from the Royal Air force in 1993 and believed that it was because she was transsexual. She made her complaint to the tribunal in 1994 well outside the 3 months' time limit.

Suggested Questions

1. What are the issues in this case?
2. What are the potential outcomes of this situation?
3. What strategies can be implemented to address this situation?

Answer

The tribunal considered that it was just and equitable to hear the claim as it had not been known at the time of the dismissal that the SDA/ETD would cover discrimination arising on the ground of being transsexual. Furthermore, as the ETD on this issue had not been transposed into domestic legislation (the SDA); the time limit had not begun to run.

NO SEARCHING ALLOWED
A v Chief Constable of the West Yorkshire Police

A underwent gender reassignment from male to female in 1996. In 1997 she applied to join West Yorkshire Police. She made it clear from the outset that she was a transsexual person and was told that, in accordance with the Force's equal opportunities policy, this would not be a problem. She was invited to continue with her application and she successfully completed the various selection tests.

However, she was then informed that since her initial application had been received, the issue of transsexual applicants had been further considered and a decision had been made that transsexual people would not be appointed to the Force.

The Force argued that as a transsexual person, A would be unable to conduct intimate and body searches of suspects, and could not therefore comply with the full range of policing functions. (The Police and Criminal Evidence Act requires that suspects are searched by a police officer of the same sex).

Suggested Questions

1. What are the issues in this case?
2. What are the potential outcomes of this situation?
3. What strategies can be implemented to address this situation?

Answer

The case reached the House of Lords who upheld a previous ruling by the Court of Appeal that to refuse A's application was contrary to the Sex Discrimination Act.

GENDER REASSIGNMENT
Fortnum v Suffolk County Council

Ms Fortnum (a male to female transsexual person) was employed as an assistant day care officer who was required to give occasional intimate personal care to the male and female day centre clients. In May 1999, the Council told her that she could no longer continue to provide this intimate personal care to one of the female clients with learning difficulties whom she dealt with as the client's mother had asked that her daughter be cared for only by female staff. The client and her mother were unaware of Ms Fortnum's gender reassignment. The Council had taken the view that as Ms Fortnum was, at that time pre-operative, she was not a woman.

Suggested Questions

1. What are the issues in this case?
2. What are the potential outcomes of this situation?
3. What strategies can be implemented to address this situation?

Answer

The tribunal considered that the Council's reliance on a genuine occupational qualification - that these services could not be provided effectively by someone undergoing gender reassignment

(Section 7B(2)(d)) was problematic as Ms Fortnum had been providing these services effectively to the client for some time before being told not to do so. There was no evidence to show that the Council had addressed the issue of whether or not the service could be provided effectively by Ms Fortnum. Her claim was successful.

RACISM

FACE DIDN'T FIT

Claire was working as a full time cashier at a petrol station run by a multinational firm, when the garage was sold to another company. The contract stated that all nine staff members would be transferred to the new employer. One day, when she arrived at work for her usual shift, Claire and her colleagues were not given any work to do as their new boss had brought in two new staff. Another staff member turned up for work to find that someone else appeared to have been given her job, so she left. A few days later, a meeting was arranged to resolve the matter, but their employer told them that they would not be paid as he could not afford it. Eventually he agreed to pay some of the wages and they went home, not knowing whether or not the garage would re-open. Two staff found work elsewhere.

Claire called the petrol station and was told to come back to work the next day, but five of the original staff were never contacted again. They felt they had been mistreated. When she returned to work she found out that her boss had hired a new manager and two new staff, all of whom were Asian. Although she got on well with her new colleagues, she felt it was unacceptable that the company had replaced the original white staff with new Asian staff. She was eventually told that she was no longer needed at the garage, and went to her local race equality service for advice.

The CRE later took up her case and her employer could not explain why he dismissed the white staff to employ family members, or only those from his ethnic group.

Suggested Questions

1. What are the issues in this case?
2. What are the potential outcomes of this situation?
3. What strategies can be implemented to address this situation?

Decision

An employment tribunal ruled that she had been racially discriminated against, and ordered the firm to pay a four figure sum to compensate for her lost earnings.

PSYCHOMETRIC TESTING AND RACISM

Sangita had been working for a public sector employer in Lancashire on a casual basis for a number of years when she was asked to take a written aptitude test in order to remain in employment.   She failed the test but later found out that a number of white employees in the same situation were given temporary or permanent contracts without having to take a test. Two of these staff were relatives of management staff.

The circumstances where the test was applied did not appear to follow any clear sequence. Sangita was concerned about this and made a complaint to her manager, who failed to investigate the matter fully. Sangita came to the CRE for advice and assistance, and we supported her case at the employment tribunal.

The tribunal stated that they had not seen any evidence of the employer's equal opportunities policy being implemented on a day to day basis. They found that the manager involved was not racist by nature, but that her failure to deal with the problem was indicative of the attitude of the organisation in dealing with legitimate complaints of discrimination.

They stated that they were concerned about the way Asian employees were treated, including Sangita, who is of Indian origin. They concluded that management had not provided a satisfactory explanation for dismissing Sangita, which led them to conclude that she had been discriminated on the grounds of her race.

Suggested Questions

1. What are the issues in this case?

2. What are the potential outcomes of this situation?

3. What strategies can be implemented to address this situation?

Decision

The tribunal confirmed that Sangita had suffered considerable distress as a result of the discrimination and stated that they had paid particular attention to the fact that the employer had blatantly refused to investigate her complaint, and that no apology had been received. The employer was ordered to pay a five figure sum in damages. This figure took account of loss of earnings, injury to feelings, and interest.

LAZY ASIAN

Ms Velagapudi (the Complainant) was an Indian migrant, and is an Australian citizen. She alleged that Ms Spooner, a co-worker at Symbion Pharmacy Services Pty Ltd (formerly Faulding HealthCare Pty Ltd), called her a "lazy, black, Indian bitch", which caused her to be distressed and humiliated, because all the warehouse employees knew about it. She complained to the management who ordered an apology and also issued a warning that dismissal would follow any repetition of the remark.

Ms Velagapudi was dissatisfied, because she believed that the apology was not genuine, and she therefore refused to accept it. She was of the view that Ms Spooner's employment should have been terminated.

She also claimed that, following her complaint, she was victimised by other employees, particularly by her new supervisor who was appointed after her complaint was made and who was Ms Spooner's boyfriend. Ms Velagapudi complained claiming race discrimination and victimisation.

Suggested Questions

1. What are the issues in this case?
2. What are the potential outcomes of this situation?
3. What strategies can be implemented to address this situation?

Solution

The content of the apology and the manner of its delivery were less than satisfactory. The awareness of Ms Spooner's boyfriend as the Complainant's supervisor, subsequent to the complaint showed "insensitivity and lack of awareness" by management; A suggestion by a manager that the Complainant attempt "to make a friendship with Ms Spooner and (her boyfriend, the new supervisor) was considered inappropriate; and There was insufficient evidence of a causal link between the alleged victimisation and the complaint of discrimination.

ALL LEBANESE MEN ARE TROUBLE

Hassan, an 18 year old male of Lebanese descent, starts work at a local supermarket. After working there for a few weeks stacking shelves he overhears the store manager telling his supervisor that "all Lebanese guys are troublemakers. I'm worried that he'll cause problems for the Aussie girls if he gets near them". After that, his supervisor tells Hassan to stay out the back of the store, where it's hot and dusty, and not talk to anyone. Hassan's supervisor and the store manager constantly watch him, and tell him off every time they catch him talking to a female member of staff. Hassan notices that none of the other male staff are treated like this when they talk to female staff members. When he asks his supervisor why he had to stay out the back while others get to stack shelves, his supervisor says that it's because he talks too much. Hassan argues with this, and points out that he didn't talk much at all when he was stacking shelves. After that, his shifts are cut.

Suggested Questions

1. What are the issues in this case?

2. What are the potential outcomes of this situation?

3. What strategies can be implemented to address this situation?

EFFECT OF RACIAL BIAS

An African American student on the trauma surgery service is hurriedly sent to perform a discharge physical on a patient the student about whom has been told nothing. The student enters the patient's room to start the physical without first reading the patient's chart, and finds upon entering that the patient is an African American male whose right arm and shoulder are bandaged. Giving the student his history, the man says that he was in a car accident.

As the student concludes his interview and begins to examine the patient, a team of Caucasian male orthopedic surgeons enters the room. Without acknowledging either the student or the patient, they approach the patient and manipulate his shoulder to determine its range of motion.

Informing the patient that he should call to schedule an orthopedics appointment next week, the chief surgeon assures the patient that, "These gunshot wounds always heal fast," and then leaves. The student feels that he should be furious with the orthopedic surgeons, and almost corrects them, but then wonders whether the man has lied to him. The student excuses himself to go read the patient's chart, which documents the man's car accident.

Possible Questions for Discussion:

1. Why might the student have been furious with the surgeons initially? How might the student have felt towards the surgeons after reading the chart?

2. Would the student's anger be less justified if the incident had occurred in a busy inner city hospital that admits many minorities secondary to violent trauma? Would his anger be more justified if the incident had occurred in a suburban community hospital that admits few minorities?

3. How might the student have felt towards himself after reading the chart? Why might he have doubted the patient?

4. Is the student's failure to read the chart before seeing the patient evidence of poor clinical skills?

5. How should the student have dealt with the surgeons? Should he have spoken to them directly? How might the student's response to the surgeons have affected the patient?

MISINFORMATION

While preparing to get her microscope and slide set to study for a histopathology test, an African-American student enters her assigned lab to find a small group of Asian American and Caucasian American students studying slides from a projector. Inviting herself to join the group, she sits down while the group's apparent leader, a talkative and friendly Caucasian American male, leads the discussion. Being a late arrival, the African-American American student sits quietly and watches the other students identify the slides.

Although there is some debate, the other students seem to differ to whomever speaks most authoritatively. As the other students get stumped by one of the slides, the African-American student volunteers what she is certain is the right answer. To her surprise, the group leader says he's got to look it up.

Asking him why he feels the need to look up her answer but no one else's, he says, "We should know the answer. We all went to top ten schools for undergrad." Packing up her microscope, she says, "Too bad you don't know how to recognize the **right answer**."

Possible Questions for Discussion:

1. Does the African-American student seem excessively offended? Does she seem justifiably offended?

2. How do you think the European American student leading the discussion feels about this exchange?

3. How do you think the other students in the room feels about this exchange? How might they describe it to their friends?

4. How do you feel about this exchange? Would it change your impression to know that the African-American student rarely has her answers challenged? Would it change your impression to know that this student and her friends feel that they're always having their answers challenged?

5. Did you make any assumptions about who her friends might be as you considered the preceding question? Is there any relationship between your assumptions about who her friends might be and the group leader's assumption that her answer was untrustworthy?

STEREOTYPICAL ASSUMPTION

An African American M.D., Ph.D. student attending a conference on binary fission in bacteria unexpectedly bumps into two of his classmates, an engaged European American couple whose parents are well-known faculty members at the school the students attend. In response to the African-American student's surprise at their attendance, the female member of the couple says that her father found grant money to pay for the couple's attendance, and that he's lined the couple up with research positions for the next year. At this, the African American express's interest in bringing a proposal to the woman's father, to whom she says, "What are you worried about? Minorities get all the cushy research positions, anyway."

Possible Questions for Discussion:

If you were the European American woman, would you take advantage of your familial connections in the same way that she apparently does? Why or why not?

1. Were the African- American man to be in the position to grant opportunities like the ones described above, how should he grant them? Should he give opportunities to his family members and acquaintances? Do you think that medical professionals in general have a tendency to grant opportunities to those whom they know?

2. Are there any similarities between the opportunities the students like African-American man may receive through affirmative action programs and the opportunities students like the European American woman receive through personal contacts? Are there any differences between the opportunities the two aforementioned groups of students receive?

3. Are the qualifications of the medical students who are children of faculty members questioned to the same degree that the qualifications of minority students sometimes are?

4. How should the African American student react? What should he say to these two classmates?

5. Assuming that the woman's father is a famous researcher with whom the African American student has been eager to work, how might he react to the woman? Why?

WHO ARE YOU CALLING "BOY"?

A Black female was the primary nurse for two black teenagers. When one got out of line, she would simply say, "Boy, keep your mouth shut and go somewhere and sit down." They usually complied. One day, it was time for one of them to go to physical therapy, but he was giving the Anglo nurse a hard time. Finally she tried the primary nurses' tactic and said "Come on boy, I'm not kidding with you. You have to go to therapy." The young man flew into a rage and started swearing at the nurse. The Anglo nurse was confused, he had never responded that way to his primary nurse.

Suggested Questions

1. What are the issues in this case?
2. What are the potential outcomes of this situation?
3. What strategies can be implemented to address this situation?

Solution

She had not considered that the term "boy" is inoffensive when used by one Black person speaking to another but is highly insulting when used by Caucasians because of its origins among slave owners.

MY FIRST NAME

Mary Smith, an elderly Black woman, was in the recovery room after surgery. To assess her condition, the nurse, spoke her name, "Mary." The patient slowly opened her eyes and turned her head but made no further signs of acknowledgment. The nurse became concerned because most patients responded readily and clearly at this point. She called the woman Mrs. Smith. She then became alert, pleasant, and cooperative.

The Issue

The patient had perceived the use of her first name as a lack of respect and a form of racism. Nurses should refer to all adult patients as Mr., Miss, Ms., or Mrs., unless otherwise instructed.

1. Can you identify where the perception of racism came from?
2. Do you think the nurse was being racist or do you think the patient just being sensitive?
3. Is it fair to assume, that the use of a first name other than by that of a close friend is both inappropriate and discourteous in most cultures?

HE AINT NO DOG

The patient was a nine-month-old Black male. His hands and feet were tied to the bed to prevent him from pulling out the intravenous lines. When his grandmother saw him tied down, she became very angry. "How come you got the baby tied down? He's not doing anything. He isn't no trouble. He ain't no dog!"

The Issue

She had experienced much discrimination at the hands of whites and perceived her grandson's treatment as a racist act. Once the nurse explained the purpose of tying the baby down, she relaxed.

Suggested Questions

1. What are the issues in this case?
2. What are the potential outcomes of this situation?
3. What strategies can be implemented to address this situation?

SEXUALITY

PARENTAL STATUS

Facts

A gay man alleged lawful sexual activity and parental status discrimination while employed with a retailer. He claimed he was subjected to numerous taunts, remarks and lurid suggestions relating to his sexual activity, from management as well as co-workers. He also said he was called derogatory names over the loud-speaker and that regularly he would find items for sale, arranged to mock his sexual preference.

The man also said when he had applied to work in the specialist children's section; he was unsuccessful in gaining the position because he was not a parent. He said he was forced to resign.

The retailer denied the allegations and counter claimed that the man openly discussed his sexual activities in the work place, which offended some staff and clients, and that the man's work performance had diminished over the three years he was employed. The retailer also denied telling him the other job needed a worker who was a parent.

Suggested Questions

1. What are the issues in this case?

2. What are the potential outcomes of this situation?

3. What strategies can be implemented to address this situation?

Decision

The matter was resolved at conciliation with the retail store agreeing to pay the man $12,500 in general damages, providing a statement of regret and statement of service to the man, and an assurance that all staff would be retrained on anti-discrimination and sexual harassment legislation.

HOMOPHOBIA

Facts

A woman alleged she was sacked by her employer because she was a lesbian. The respondent found it offensive that she and her partner had once held hands when they left his premises and he had also written religious quotes condemning homosexuality in a book she was reading. He cited work performance and claimed her replacement was a better worker.

Suggested Questions

1. What are the issues in this case?
2. What are the potential outcomes of this situation?
3. What strategies can be implemented to address this situation?

Decision

He agreed that he did not like the fact that she was a lesbian but maintained that it was not the reason she was sacked.

DISCLOSURE

In a supervised session an employee expresses a concern to you. They have recently disclosed their sexuality to a fellow collect who they have always got on well with. Their colleague was surprised and stated that they have a strong moral objection to lesbians and gay men.

They recognised the need to treat others with respect regardless of their sexuality, so while they felt it was not acceptable to be a lesbian they nevertheless wanted to maintain a positive relationship with their colleague.

They requested that the lesbian employee should help in this by not referring greatly to their sexuality again.

- Is this response acceptable?

Issues/principles

We always want to respect the values and perspective of others. However, in this context there are certain 'non-negotiables' we need to consider. Students are required to treat all people with respect. This includes course colleagues, tutors and patients, regardless of any aspect of their social identity.

Your organisation has an equality policy which covers all employees and students and requires them not to discriminate on any aspect of social identity including sexuality. Refusing to acknowledge their colleague's sexuality could be considered discriminatory.

There is a legal framework around sexuality that would prevent an individual directly treating someone less favourably on the grounds of their sexuality.

As a practical way forward you may want to meet with the individual and discuss your concerns with them and your expectations regarding their future behaviour.

HOMOPHOBIC ABUSE

During a work based training session, a religious trainer describes homosexuality as 'unnatural' and 'depraved' and states that he has no issue in covering diversity issue but anything to do with homosexuality and transgender issue will not be addressed. A bisexual pupil in the class is upset and offended by these comments. As harassment doesn't apply to the protected characteristic of sexual orientation in schools, this is likely to be unlawful direct discrimination because of sexual orientation.

Suggested Questions

1. What are the issues in this case?
2. What are the potential outcomes of this situation?
3. What strategies can be implemented to address this situation?

DON'T TELL!

A pupil who is gay is offered a place at an independent school on the condition that he hides his sexual orientation and pretends that he is straight (heterosexual). This is likely to be unlawful direct discrimination because of sexual orientation.

1. What are the issues in this case?
2. What are the potential outcomes of this situation?
3. What strategies can be implemented to address this situation?

IT'S JUST FUN!

A sixth form pupil is bullied for being bisexual and although he reports the bullying to a teacher no action is taken as the teacher believes that it is just a bit of banter and he deserves 'some teasing' if he is going to say he is bisexual. This is likely to be unlawful direct discrimination because of sexual orientation, rather than harassment.

Suggested Questions

1. What are the issues in this case?

2. What are the potential outcomes of this situation?

3. What strategies can be implemented to address this situation?

CROSS DRESSER

One of the senior employees has come to you with a problem he's recently discovered with an employee. The employee is one of the top performers in the group, is always on time and has never had problems on the job. However, the senior employee has recently learned that this man is a cross-dresser and often goes out in public dressed in make-up, a wig, and women's clothing. The employee is a company truck driver and so has contact with the public while on the job. To the senior employee's knowledge, the employee has never cross-dressed at work, but in the interest of protecting the company's image, would like to see his employment terminated.

You are a group of employee relations team members working for Walgreens pharmacy. Your task today is to address an issue (described ABOVE) that has come up.

Suggested Questions

1. What are the issues in this case?
2. What are the potential outcomes of this situation?
3. What strategies can be implemented to address this situation?

BE IT BUT DON'T FLAUNT IT!

Self-directed work teams have been established to work on a number of new projects. Kofi, a member of one the new work teams, recently spoke with his supervisor about his team. His supervisor has come to you for help. Kofi says he is a "fundamentalist Christian" with strong religious beliefs. He expresses concern about Paul, one of the members of his team. Paula is openly gay. She keeps a small picture of her partner of ten years at her workstation. Kofi is having a hard time accepting the fact that he has to work with Paula. He has stated that she "flaunts her immoral lifestyle for all to see" (referring to the partner's picture). He asks to be removed from the project immediately. Both Kofi and Paula have critical skill sets needed for the project to succeed.

You are a group of employee relations team members in a large A& E clinic. Your task today is to address an issue (described below) that has come up.

You must:

1. Identify The Diversity Issues In The Scenario
2. Discuss Possible Solutions To The Problem
3. Briefly Describe Your Issues And Solutions To The Class.

ADVERTISEMENTS

A night club advertises its services on some flyers as follows:

1. Come to the best nightclub in town!

2. Over 21s only.

3. Ladies – you'll get two for one on drinks all night on Tuesdays.

4. Gents – no groups of 3 or more men admitted without accompanying ladies.

5. No hoodies or other head coverings allowed – just don't bother as you won't get in!

6. English must be spoken – we'll be checking!

7. Please note – our venue is unsuitable for pregnant women and disabled people.

Question: **What is wrong with this advertisement?**

Please list the wording which you think may unlawfully discriminate and say what is wrong with it.

Answer

Over 21s only: no problem with this at the moment. After 2011, the club will need to be able to justify this direct age discrimination.

Ladies – you'll get two for one on drinks all night on Tuesdays: this may well be unlawful direct discrimination because of sex – men are being treated worse just because they are men.

Gents – no groups of 3 or more men admitted without accompanying ladies: this is direct sex discrimination – groups of 3 women are allowed in but groups of 3 men are not, just because they are men.

No hoodies or other head coverings allowed: this discriminates against people of a number of religions who are required to wear a head covering, such as Muslims, observant Jews, Sikhs and Rastafarians. It would be unlawful unless it could be justified as a balanced way of achieving a worthwhile outcome (a proportionate means to a legitimate end).

English must be spoken: this is more likely to put people who cannot speak English at a disadvantage compared to people who speak English so is potentially indirect discrimination because of race – also some disabled people may be affected, for example, British Sign Language users or people with a severe speech impediment may not pass the declared check. It would be unlawful unless it could be justified as serving a legitimate aim (a proportionate means to a legitimate end). Altering this rule for disabled people who are affected by it may well in any event be a reasonable adjustment.

Our venue is unsuitable for pregnant women and disabled people: this blanket declaration could be unfavourable treatment of pregnant women or direct discrimination because of disability. It would not be pregnancy discrimination if the club could show that it is necessary to exclude pregnant women on ground of health or safety (which would bring them within a permitted exception), but they would need to provide evidence of this. For disability, it is not possible to make a blanket statement against disabled people as an entire group as there is such a range of impairments. So this wording is definitely unlawful. Because the club seeks to deny access to disabled people then it is likely that it would also be acting unlawfully as it is unlikely to be prepared to make reasonable adjustments.

DISMISSAL

A large organisation has had some problems recently and its equality policies have been inconsistently applied. Managers have been told to make sure that staff are 'kept up to the mark' for attendance and discipline and to take disciplinary action as necessary, including dismissing anyone who has reached their limit of oral and written warnings for misconduct. When a new manager arrives, there are four employees in their department who are in this position:

Terry is a 50 year old white British man. He has sometimes shouted at fellow workers and even at the previous manager, for which he was disciplined. He says his loss of temper is because of the pain he experiences from a long-term disability (a back condition).

Shireen is a 30 year old British Asian woman who has consistently ignored the dress code and been disciplined for this. She says that as a devout Muslim, she cannot wear her shirt tucked into her trousers because this would be immodest.

Sarah is a 24 year old openly gay white British woman who has missed several **deadlines for finishing work. She has said she just could not fit everything in.**

Richard is a 37 year old black British man. Before the new manager arrived, he had helped a colleague with a complaint that the colleague was being sexually harassed by a different manager. D has been disciplined for unrelated matters.

Question: *Looking at this just in terms of equality law (rather than any wider management issues), is it unlawful to dismiss any of these employees? If so, which?*

www.ingramcontent.com/pod-product-compliance
Lightning Source LLC
Chambersburg PA
CBHW080307290526
45790CB00005B/1962